RUN YOUR RACE

RUN YOUR RACE

HOW TO KEEP GOING WHEN LIFE WEARS YOU OUT

ELLE BABINGTON STEELE

First Edition: February 2014

ISBN 978-0-9914169-0-5 / ISBN 978-0-9914169-1-2 (eBook)

Contact (booking@ebabingtonsteele.com) to book the author
for a speaking event.

Library of Congress Control Number: 2014901041

Printed in the United States of America

This book is dedicated to all of the people whose dreams have been deferred and whose journeys have felt like marathons; to my family of fighters (Mom, Dad, Z, D, & Bobby) for allowing me to share your stories as a message of hope; to my father, who many years ago, and even still, tells me "run your race"; to my beautiful angel, Dakota Sky, who is forever smiling down on us; to Dominic, our gift from the Lord that is sure to come; and to my soul mate Dwayne—my light, my love, and my friend.

CONTENTS

FOREWORD

Some truths of life are revealed as we make this journey from time to eternity. One that is demonstrated in every time zone and culture is the power wielded by pressures of various kinds that, if allowed, would mold us and direct (or redirect) us. Certainly peer pressure is one of the leading culprits that rob young and old alike of their uniqueness. A crowd personality emerges from a place that an individual used to dwell.

External pressures attack, but often the most challenging sources that exert the force that results in hasty decisions and not very-well-thought out courses of action come from within. We could label these doubts, fears, or insecurities. Our esteem for ourselves or our lack of confidence in our abilities, particularly as we do comparisons to what we assume about others that are around us, can be crippling.

One of the greatest gifts we can receive is that which will empower us to take on life with courage, to honor what we have, and to strive earnestly to reach all that we are capable of achieving. This volume you have in your hands or have downloaded onto some twenty-first-century device is such a gift.

The title *Run Your Race* may seem elementary, but I want to assure you that if you truly understand and embrace the message, you will find it to be elegant in its simplicity and empowering because of the truth it offers. The phrase has become an important landmark in our family story. These words were launched from my spirit, through my vocal cords, and out of my mouth one day, directed at my daughter. She was demonstrating an iron will as part of her character and taking on physical and emotional challenges in a public setting, which you will learn more of in the pages that follow. I saw her inner strength and determination, and I wanted to affirm and encourage her. I shouted to her, "RUN YOUR RACE, MUNCH! RUN YOUR RACE!" I often describe my daughter as the best human being I know. As you engage with this important book, I believe you will better understand why I consider her a godly asset, and I believe you will find the power to run your race as well.

Alfred Babington-Johnson
Author's father

INTRODUCTION
"RUN YOUR RACE!"

About twenty or so years ago I was about to run the race of my life. This race was not a figurative one, but literally a race in which I qualified to run at the regional level in the Junior Olympics (having advanced past the state level). Why the race of my life? We will get to that a little later. As a young girl, I was what many would consider to be skinny and awkward, given my lanky appearance and developing coordination. I was, by all accounts, one who was not predicted to advance past the regional level, and as it turns out, I didn't. However, I had by some display of ability earned my spot to run in this race. It is important to note that I was placed in a lane toward the outside of the track (lane eight or nine). Thus, it was fair to say that the odds may have been stacked against me, as it was common knowledge which lanes were assigned to those that had the best qualifying times (lanes four and five). Regardless, I was at the starting line for the 800-meter dash (two laps around the track). As I entered my lane, I got into position (one knee set on the track beneath me, the other set in the air ready to begin the race). Upon the bang of the starting gun I took off. I applied the running approach I was given by my coaches in the past (pace yourself). I started slow to maintain my endurance for the entire race. Strategies aside, soon after I began running, it appeared very quickly that my competitors were pulling ahead. By my first lap I was well behind everyone in the race. However, I continued to run. As my race continued, my competitors crossed the finish line. I still had three-quarters of my last lap yet to complete. Now alone on the track, it would no longer be possible for me to win or even qualify for the finals. However, I continued to run. Running now not a race for the win or for qualification, but a race to finish.

As I was getting closer to completing the race, I remembered my coaches instructing me in times past to finish strong by applying a sprint finish. I may have taken a very long time to run this race, but I had conserved enough energy to kick things into high gear at the end. I began to pick up my speed with sheer will and ferocity. My determination was consistent with one who still had a chance of finishing first or qualifying for the finals. As I zeroed in on my last hundred meters, I was in a full sprint. Much to my surprise, the crowd cheered as I ran toward the finish line. My father shouted from the stands with great spirit, telling me, "RUN YOUR RACE, MUNCH!" ("Munch" is a term of endearment my father uses to refer to me.) And I did. I ran my race all the way to the end.

Why was it my race? It was my race because it was no longer the conventional win I was running for; it was my race because I decided to run until I, too, crossed that finish line, in spite of where I placed. Why was it the race of my life? It was the race of my life because, as fate would have it, many of the experiences I would live through in my life would show me that I might not be the one to cross many of life's proverbial finish lines first, but my determination and drive would allow me to keep going until the end.

If you are reading this book and looking to get encouragement from the perspective of a person who is used to crossing the finish line first, figuratively speaking, you should probably put this book down and find another. I am quite accustomed to not finishing first. Actually, I often finish last. So I wrote this book for those who have gone through life and feel as if they have somehow missed out on winning. I wrote this book for those who may have had some wins, but were devastated by a really big loss. I wrote this book for those who have been overlooked, underestimated, and misunderstood. I wrote this book for those of you who have been made to feel worthless at many of life's turns and bends, because you haven't quite gotten a return on all of the effort and energy you put out there to accomplish your dreams, hopes, and aspirations. I wrote this book to inspire you to keep going in spite of the challenges and heartbreak you may be experiencing. I wrote this book for you and for myself. I am currently going through one of the hardest, most painful moments of my life. This book is a compilation of my thoughts, revelations, and stories that I tell of those who kept going in spite of whatever came their way. I use all of this to keep me going. I am in the midst of trying to achieve what I hope will be my first successful pregnancy (you will read the full story later on in the book). I wrestle daily with an overlooked and poorly researched neurological sensory disorder that challenges my interactions and experiences on a moment-to-moment basis. It is sometimes debilitating. There are a number of other challenging circumstances I could share about my life that few people know, but my personal story is not the point of this book. I do not share these circumstances for pity, nor to convey that I have been dealt the worst hand. I know there are many who have far worse circumstances than I. I also know there are many who have far less blessings than God has bestowed upon me. I know there are so many that suffer in silence. I only share some of my challenges to give you the perspective that I write from.

The point of this book is: you can't give up. You just can't! If you do, you never get to get there. Never! If you keep going, you are always striving, using the light and energy that hopefulness brings. I believe you will get there! I believe I will! Neither of us can afford to believe anything different if we truly expect to get there at all. The only way to win is to stay in the race and to keep running. Even if it is not the current race you are running that you get to win, continuing to race at all is the only way you eventually get to your first gold medal (whatever that may be for you symbolically).

How do you keep going when life wears you out? You run your race. Running your race is about disregarding the race run by someone else; you are focused on your own end goal. Running your race is about striving towards a dream in spite of how long it may take you to achieve it. Running your race is about finishing what you start, even when you may be the one to finish last. Running your race is about the determination and will you demonstrate to keep going all the way to the end, no matter how many times you get knocked down along the way. Running your race is about continuing to keep going in spite of that which is attempting to slow you down and hinder your forward movement. So, how do you run your race? Let's start with chapter one.

ONE
FALSE START

What is a false start? In track and field, it is a term used to refer to a runner who moves before being signaled. I don't know if you have ever observed such a scenario (if you have watched races in the Olympics or at any level), but it is as if the runner heard the starting gun and took off before the trigger was pulled. Or perhaps the runner simply moved in anticipation of the trigger being pulled. Let's face it, this competitor has trained a great deal to avoid such a circumstance. Runners certainly don't engage in a false start intentionally (most of them anyway). However, the price the runner pays for such an act will not take his or her desire, preparation, or intention into account. The runner may receive a warning of disqualification or may be disqualified from the race on the first occurrence. This means that the runner, who has prepared years for this race, will be unable to compete for this gold medal in what the runner hoped would be his or her culminating moment. In my own life, I have experienced the disqualifying blows and the feeling of rejection that results from a false start. False starts can be devastating. The bottom line is, when it's not time, it just isn't time, and there is not much you can do about that. Can you relate to this notion? A false start can really throw you off. You could have used the energy you lost in the false start to finish the race ahead of you. Very rarely do you begin again with the same level of energy you started with. False starts in life force you to return to the starting point and begin all over again. This is a terribly frustrating situation that I know all too well. Let me tell you my story.

STORY | A LONG FALSE START

My husband and I had been married for five years. We believed it was finally time for us to start our family so we began trying for our first child. We didn't try by chance; we tried with strategy. Following the fertility calendar, we tried when it was deemed a fertile period and even when it was not. We remained surrendered to God's divine timing (we knew when the time was right, we would become pregnant). The first month of trying went by without success. The next month we tried again for a baby, and much to our excitement and glee we found out we were pregnant. We shared the news with our immediate family, and we looked forward to sharing our news with other loved ones and friends in the coming weeks (once we made it past our first trimester). Unfortunately, that would not happen, because four weeks later I went through an excruciating natural miscarriage. I mean three days of incomprehensible physical pain and bleeding that all led to the natural miscarriage of a baby on December 12, 2012. It was a heartbreaking experience for us.

It took some strength to believe we could continue trying. However, my mother had experienced a miscarriage prior to my birth, so I believed that I would go on to successfully have my first baby, to complete the full journey, just as my mother had. My husband and I decided to purchase a co-sleeper (it attached to the side of our bed in order to make nighttime feedings easier and bonding a priority). We purchased this co-sleeper by faith. We were not yet pregnant, but we believed we would be soon, so we continued trying for a baby (this was quite therapeutic for us).

As destiny would have it, a month later we were pregnant again with what we believed would be our first child to term. This time we were wary of sharing our pregnancy news beyond our immediate family, so we remained quiet. We tempered our excitement with the perspective we gained from our previous pregnancy and decided to wait until we got past the halfway mark in our pregnancy before we shared our news this time. We knew getting that far would indicate a favorable outcome of the pregnancy so we decided that sometime thereafter would be a better stage to share our news.

At our twenty-week ultrasound appointment, we learned of a possible clubfoot and missing bone in the lower leg of the baby inside my womb. We learned that if this turned out to be the case, there was nothing we could do about it until after the baby was born, so we maintained great faith and belief that this would not be the case. We would later learn that our baby did have these defects, but they would be the least of our worries. We continued past the halfway point and finally began buying clothing, baby bottles, diapers, toys, and so on. We did everything parents with a baby on the way dream of doing. We arranged the baby's room and finally celebrated our bundle of joy with family and friends at our baby shower. We were excited, and so were our loved ones. Our baby was due September 28, 2013.

On September 26, my water broke. I was so excited, but I wasn't quite sure why I wasn't in labor. After consulting with my midwife, I was given assurance that sometimes a woman's water breaks before she goes into labor. My midwife instructed my husband and me to simply remain relaxed and monitor for infection. Diligently, we monitored for infection by constantly taking my temperature, checking the color of the amniotic fluid, and so on. No signs of infection. Finally, late on the night of September 30, I began to go into labor. Our moment had finally come; we were near the finish line.

I had always desired to have a natural birth, and I would go on to have one. However, I had dysfunctional labor (as a result of my water breaking early), which exacerbated the pain and the duration of my labor experience. The level of agony I experienced while laboring cannot be expressed in words. For those women who intend to have a natural birth, you will likely have a much different experience than I had (please research the plethora of beautiful natural birth stories). Also remember, my labor experience was not normal or typical. By the way, kudos to all women who give birth in whatever way you choose (C-section, natural, and so on)! After twenty-nine hours of labor, our sweet baby girl, Dakota Sky, was born naturally at 12:33 a.m. on October 2, 2013. As the nurses reached for the baby, I requested that they wait to cut the cord until it stopped pulsing (I wanted to make sure everything vital had an opportunity to transfer from the placenta to our new bundle of joy). In the past, I researched the value in making this decision and decided to implement it to ensure an optimal start for our new baby's life. Very quickly my words fell on deaf ears. The nurses scurried with urgency, quickly cutting the cord and taking the baby over to the infant warmer that was in close proximity, in order to attempt to resuscitate our baby girl. I was in utter shock, taken aback by the turn of events. Unfortunately, our little angel did not make it past a few breaths.

We were blindsided by our baby's sudden death. My mother, father, brother, and husband were in the room with me, feeling disbelief and utter grief. Family and friends near and far were completely heartbroken. Early that morning my husband and I left the hospital, not with our new baby, but with a stuffed animal provided by the hospital for families in bereavement. We drove home that dark morning with an empty car seat in tow and a baby bag that no longer had use. We returned to our home only to encounter all of the visual reminders that a baby was supposed to be with us. Diapers, toys, books galore. Dreams, hopes, prayers now diminished. Not only would we endure the emotional pain and agony of such a loss, but I would still go on to experience the physical transformation that occurs as a result of having carried a baby full term and giving birth. I experienced painful engorgement from my inability to nurse. I experienced the physical discomfort associated with trying to function normally after having given birth naturally. I experienced the visceral maternal instinct to be with and protect my baby, which had no way of being satisfied. I experienced having to look at myself in the mirror and see the manifestation of life having come forth, in spite of the fact that life had now been lost. I experienced the pain of watching the love of my life grieve with a level of agony for which I could not provide comfort. It was devastating. The pain felt by my family and loved ones was palpable. Our hearts were broken beyond belief.

The day after Dakota's death was my birthday.

My husband and I spent the day making funeral arrangements at the funeral home. That very same day we were told that as a result of Dakota's birth defects, she would have to be cremated immediately. We were shocked that this would be our final moment to say good-bye to her in this form (we wanted to have an open casket funeral so our loved ones could see our daughter and say their good-byes). Utterly devastated, my brother, my husband, and I spent my birthday holding our deceased baby girl while saying our farewells. Our other loved ones lived too far away to arrive soon enough to say good-bye in this way. As the days continued, the blows kept coming. From the heartbreaking autopsy reports to a number of other challenges that resulted from our angel's life and sudden death, my husband and I felt as if life was no longer worth living.

How is that for a false start? It is important for me to state that I have not spelled out all of the details of this story, as it is not most important for this book, but know that the medical staff involved, the midwife, my husband, and I did everything we knew to do at the time to facilitate what we all hoped would be a successful end to a beautiful pregnancy. Let me also share that I know there are women who have had far more debilitating pregnancy and birth experiences than mine. There are women who have had longer journeys to even becoming pregnant. There are some who have never had the opportunity to carry a child in their womb, even though it was their desire, and they may have tried tirelessly to do so. I honor all of you and your journeys. My point in sharing my story is to let you know what we are doing now, a couple months after the passing of our daughter, Dakota Sky. After doctor's appointments, tests, lots and lots of questions to the medical staff, crying, screaming, mourning, yearning, and praying we have decided to try again for a baby. We decided to begin this race again. We are trying again for a baby that we pray will make it past a few breaths. We are trying again for a child who gets to live a full and beautiful life. The point in all of this is that we are continuing to try. The only way we get to have another baby is to get back in the race.

No, at this point of the story, I have not gone on to have a child who makes it. When we are at this stage in life, we don't always know what God's answer will be. I am sharing from the perspective of someone still running the race. Perhaps you, too, are journeying toward something you have not yet achieved. Perhaps you, too, are frustrated by a false start in your life. Are you recovering from an addiction, but just relapsed? Have you been divorced—once, twice, three times or more? Did you just get out of a bad relationship, but you thought this one was the one? Perhaps you were recently laid off or fired, and now you have to find a new job. Perhaps you had to spend your entire savings on an unexpected expense. Perhaps you just received word that your cancer came back after treatments and chemotherapy and being told it was in remission.

What is it in your life that may have started, but has now come to a sudden stop? What is it for you that you thought would turn out one way, and it went another? What in your life took energy, money, time, prayers, and devotion out of you and led you right back to the starting point? Whatever it may be, I encourage you to do this one thing: keep your eyes on the prize. Know that striving toward it is the only way to get to it. Absolutely, positively the only way. You want to get there, don't you? Of course you do. What you have to do, then, is keep your eyes on the prize. Keep going, my friend, by any means necessary. The only way my husband and I could possibly keep trying for a baby at this point is by hoping to finally have a child who lives; a child we get to share our lives with. We have leaned on the support of family and on the unwavering hand of God. We have taken time to do nothing besides bellow, holler, and groan. We have taken several respites where there was no work, no noise, just silence and each other. We have focused on our healing, and we are very clear that healing will continue to be a long journey for us, but we are back in the race. It takes a lot of mental fortitude to keep going in life when things don't always work out or, more often than not, don't work out at all. Just remember, the fact that you are still here is an indication that you have a destiny yet to fulfill. You just can't give up now. You can make it, get back in the race! So when life hands you a false start, take a deep breath and start all over again.

TWO
STAY IN YOUR LANE

Stay in your lane. What do I mean by that? I am talking about working within parameters that place you in a position to thrive and soar in a way only you can. I am talking about when you maintain a certain level of alignment that allows you to transform that which is before you and within you and take it to a place beyond what you could ever imagine. I am talking about you standing firm in who you are—the nuances of you, your character, your tendencies, your nature, your very makeup. I am talking about anchoring yourself in all of the things that you know to be most true about you and who you are. I am talking about you functioning from a place that may not be the most popular, but it is the most you. I am talking about operating from a space that has nothing to do with everyone else's idea of what you should be and what you should be striving toward, but has everything to do with your specific and unique desire and preference for your own life. It is about you being able to maneuver in a manner in which your concern is not the person on the left or the right of you. It is about you not being fixated on the journey of another, so much so that you find yourself outside your own lane. It is about that moment when you recognize that the reason some of your pursuits haven't worked out is because they were not central to your core, that which makes you exactly who you are. It is about the God-inspired passion that lies within you that you activate in order to gain a momentum impossible without you being exactly in the place destined for you and not another. It is about your ability to quiet all of the noise and chatter around you that has a tendency to influence your behaviors, decisions, and opinions. It is about having a central focus and sense of direction that makes you step over and walk around anything contrary to your desired destination.

As you are setting out on this race called life, or while you are in your respective race toward your goals and dreams, you must do two very fundamental things to stay in your lane. One, you must know who you are. Knowing who you are allows you to draw upon the qualities within you that facilitate a successful journey. These are what I like to refer to as your natural resources. Knowing your own strengths and weaknesses allows you to run your race with the highest level of intention and strategy that only this type of clarity brings about. The second thing you must do to stay in your lane is to be clear on where you are trying to go. Any direction works for the person with no destination in mind. Perhaps you have become so enamored with someone else's journey that you are inspired to try and take their path. But their path may not be for you. How effective is it to be journeying toward something that isn't for you or isn't really what you want for your own life when it's all said and done?

There are also two factors that make staying in your lane quite difficult. The first is when you judge yourself by virtue of the comparisons you make between yourself and another. Sure, people you know may very well look as if they are ahead in life. They may seem to achieve that which you are striving for with a level of ease that is not consistent with the effort that has been necessary for you to accomplish the same goal. However, focusing on their journey from your lane is bound to give you a distorted perception of reality. The second factor that makes staying in your lane difficult is the outside judgment of others. Judgment from the outside is an indication of someone else's focus being in the wrong place (perhaps they are trying to enter your lane or tell you how to run your race instead of being concerned with their own). This is difficult not only because it can be very distracting to your journey, but it can also make you feel insecure about the path you are taking. The more the questions and criticizing occur, the less comfortable you may be with the journey before you. Allow me to clarify – it is important to receive counsel from the most trusted individuals around you. It is also important for you to decipher between invaluable wisdom and disparaging criticism, and even that invaluable wisdom must be filtered through your instincts and personal preferences for your own life.

On the track each lane is beside the other. When you start off in one lane and there are runners in all of the other lanes, your biggest asset is to remain in your own. Why? Well, in many instances in track and field, you get disqualified if you leave your lane. How is it that you might become disqualified in life's proverbial race? The times when you overextend yourself financially, physically, spiritually, and otherwise so as to "keep up" with someone else, the challenges that come about as a result of those decisions may disqualify you. Being honest with yourself about who you are—your strengths, weaknesses, regrets, shortcomings, talents, and where you want to go—will allow you to work within these aspects to leverage them to your advantage. That's your lane. It is not by chance that you are who you are. My belief is that your very nature, makeup, and personality was taken into consideration when God assigned you to your path. I believe God took into account what you would have to go through or experience, and by design God crafted you specifically to be able to handle all that comes your way.

Now don't get me wrong; staying in your lane sometimes requires restraint. It requires the ability on your part to recognize where your lane starts and where it stops. It requires restraint to understand how to work within your lane versus expending any of your energy trying to do anything else. It requires an ironclad focus on how to best invest your time and energy in a way that allows you to most effectively work toward your dreams and ambitions.

Quite often I have observed the encouragement provided by television, families, churches, and others that admonishes people to not go with the crowd by using drugs, having unprotected sex, having premarital sex and so on. Growing up, I was inundated with the emphasis that was placed on not doing something just because another was doing it. That proved to be invaluable information for me, and as a result I didn't give in to many of the peer pressures that surrounded me then and even now. However, not often enough do I see encouragement given to people to be everything that they are, even if someone else may not fully understand it. Let me explain this another way. In my own life, I often found I had many people who encouraged me to not do something just because other people are doing it. However, I didn't have nearly as many people affirming me to be who I was if it didn't match their idea of what I should be. There is not a great deal of emphasis being placed on this very important area in our societal consciousness. All over the media there are examples of the judgment that is placed on people as soon as they begin to transform into someone the media had not anticipated or make a decision that is beyond convention. This person is demonized, ridiculed, and rebuked. There is a message that is consistently perpetuated that if you don't match a certain image or persona, you have now become an acceptable target for ongoing criticism and judgment. Here is what I want you to know. It takes an incredible amount of courage to be all that you are and to decide to move toward whatever your goal and vision is for your own life. I am going to tell you what few people told me: I acknowledge you for your unique ambition. Kudos to you for the individuality of your enterprise!

STAY IN YOUR LANE |
PERSONAL NOTE

I have spent a good amount of my life being misunderstood and not fully seen. As a result, I experienced a great deal of rejection and reprimanding for simply being who I was or trying to figure out life on my own terms. Having this kind of experience throughout my life (particularly as I was coming into my own) was quite painful for me. Perhaps you, too, have endured the pain that can be felt from having someone, that matters to you, disapprove of you and your choices by trying to impose their will upon you. Perhaps there are those that make degrading comments to your face or behind your back. Perhaps they make assumptions about you because they have a limited understanding of who you are and where you are headed. Let me break down this concept further by sharing my personal experience in this area in a little more detail. Amongst other things, I am a very creative person. Although we all have creativity inside of us, I am referring to creativity as a synonym for eccentric or unconventional. Eccentric human beings tend to explore clothing, hair, the arts, life, etc. in a way that it may be difficult, for those that don't share this quality, to fully understand. I often had, and still have, experiences of hearing people comment or hearing that people commented negatively on my clothing, hair, life, etc. You may be able to imagine how this makes staying in my own lane difficult, as a result of often feeling misunderstood. You may have experienced being rejected or ridiculed for something you are or for a decision you made, that has nothing to do with creativity, but you had the same difficulty staying in your lane as a result of the criticism you received. This attribute or decision makes you more vulnerable to being mocked or questioned. All of this chatter makes it hard to focus on the road ahead and certainly makes it difficult to feel confident proceeding forward as your own human being. I am taking this moment to advocate for those of you that may be just like me or have been made to feel the way I have been made to feel. I know first hand the frustration and pain associated with this type of chatter. The chatter I am addressing is the noise that distracts you and makes you question yourself altogether. The images perpetuated on the television, in magazines, etc. that make you feel inadequate. I am addressing the negative conversations about you that occur without your presence, that you later hear about. The vicious statements that are made to your face and behind your back. This is the stuff I know first hand. This is when it can be very difficult to stay in your lane. What do I recommend you do about all of that? I recommend you shut out all of the chatter! Quiet all of the noise. This has helped me to continue on my journey without regard for the naysayers (but I am still a work in progress). Here are some suggestions of how you can go about shutting out the chatter:

- *Thoughtfully decide who you interact with.* You

should not only be mindful of who you decide to be around, but also of what you watch, read, listen to, etc. Is who or what you have surrounding you helping or hurting you?

- *Carefully determine how much personal information you offer to those that don't have your best interest in mind or to those most critical of you.* The less you share, the less you tend to hear—this includes how you interact or engage on social media.

- *Ignore the disparaging remarks.* Brush them right off of your shoulders with grace. You are not going to be able to avoid hearing or seeing things that are negative, but you can decide how much power you give them.

- *Focus on positive images, people, etc. that reinforce*

your unique attributes or decisions. Instead of your focus being in a place that perpetuates the noise, empower yourself through messaging that helps you feel more confident about your unique attributes, decisions, etc.

In order to embark on your journey and not find yourself doing something just because it would create less controversy (more people would like you or less people would have something to say about it), you must disregard the noise and remain focused on operating from a place of authenticity. You owe that to yourself! There very well may be something about you that tends to set alarms off for people around you. But, so what! In truth, at some point you may find that it doesn't matter what you do, there will always be commentary circulating around you (someone always manages to be outside of their own lane). All you can control is how much energy you give it. So disregard all of the noise and chatter. Don't listen to it or give it any power—don't internalize it. Proceed forward with the clarity and focus staying in your lane requires and keep striving towards your goals. Use the pain and frustration that comes from having these experiences (being mocked, ridiculed, etc.) as fuel to set fire to your drive towards that which you are working to achieve. Arriving at your goal will make everything you endured worth it in the end.

Stay focused, my people. Stay in your lane by not striving for something that would not truly be fulfilling and satisfying to you in exchange for all your effort. Pursue that which is innate within you. Pursue that which is organic to you, your quirks, that which makes you who you are. Make sure that which you are working toward is what you really want for your life and is central to who you are at your core. Remember to quiet all of the chatter and that which distracts from the road ahead. Stay in your lane, my friend. Your own lane leads you to the gold medal that has been waiting for you, and only you, from day one.

THREE
INSIDE TRACK

The inside track refers to the athlete on the inside track lane having an advantage over others in the other lanes because that person's journey ends up being shorter. So what does the inside track have to do with you? Well, let's look at the inside track another way. The inside track in its non-sports-related usage refers to a person who has extra information about a specific area. Is there any specific area you happen to know a little more about than the average person? This can be anything. Maybe it's food, sports, or cultivating relationships, but there is something that it is safe to say you are an expert in one way or another, regardless of how insignificant you may deem it. Staying in your lane and knowing who you are will provide you insight into where you are strong or proficient—that is your inside track. Sure, there are areas in which you may feel you are behind, but the way to make it to the finish line is to understand where you make it out ahead. This will help to carry you forward. Not only so, it will help you to understand how life balances everything out. You see, where on the one hand you may have connected to where you are weak, there is another area where you are strong that you may not have connected to or fully embraced yet.

It is also important to note that it is not just

your strengths that put you on the inside track, but also your weaknesses. Sometimes where you come up short ends up leading you through another door with a level of ease made possible only through the opportunity the weakness produces. You should sit with that thought for a bit. It may allow you to look at your setbacks and shortcomings differently; so identify where you are on the inside track. This allows you to leverage whatever that thing may be. Once you identify your inside track, work that thing until the wheels fall of it! Let me illustrate this concept with a story.

STORY | A MAN WHO WORKED HIS INSIDE TRACK

I once knew a man who was pursuing a medical degree from Georgetown University School of

Medicine. His entry into this institution was no simple feat. While others may have gained entry into this prestigious medical school by outstanding academics and test scores, this young man's entry into the school ended up being less conventional. After he submitted his medical school application to a number of noteworthy medical schools, he did not gain acceptance to any. Now, let me be clear – this young man had an exceptional academic background and great test scores and recommendations. He had even received a tuition scholarship at his undergraduate institution (Howard University) as a result of his strong academic performance. However, this young man would end up taking the longer route to get into one of his dream schools. After not being accepted to any medical schools, he decided to look for another way in. He applied and gained entry into the post-baccalaureate Georgetown Experimental Medical Studies (GEMS) Program. This was a year-long program that helped to better prepare an individual for the rigors and stress that medical school demands. After he completed that year, that young man reapplied and was granted entry into Georgetown University School of Medicine. Where is the inside track in that story? He used his inability to gain entry the conventional way as a tool to gain entry in the less conventional way, and he still got to the same place. Because he established relationships and rapport with Georgetown University School of Medicine faculty during his post-baccalaureate year, once he reapplied and went on interviews he was now a familiar face and name. They knew firsthand the drive, determination, and intellect of this person they had come to know over the course of that post-bac year.

And guess what? That man happens to be my husband! He worked his inside track and got accepted. Yes, it took determination and dedication, but these are qualities that he has demonstrated throughout the course of his life during other very trying situations and obstacles. His inside track not only turned out to be his post-bac year, but also the conditioning and endurance he had gained in life that facilitated his willingness to look for another way into medical school, after initially not being accepted.

You see my point? No, he didn't get to his goal via the conventional route, but his being denied entry placed him on a different path. His taking the extra time to prepare himself for medical school ended up being the vehicle upon which he got in. So what is your inside track? What is it in your life that you may be perceiving in the wrong way, and thus are unable to use it to your advantage? You can work that thing to bring you close to your goal. Not only so, your strengths will get you there. But how often do you perceive your weaknesses as strengths?

Let's do a little exercise. Grab a piece of paper and a pen or pencil. Now create a list of all of your strengths on the left side of that paper and put all of your weaknesses on the right side of the paper. Now, cut or tear that piece of paper down the middle and attach your weaknesses to the strength side of the paper. Your weaknesses only get to be weaknesses if you don't know how to leverage them. Now I want you to write down an advantage to each weakness. I don't care what it is, write it down. For instance, if you continue to be denied, consider for a moment the tenacity it is creating within you. Perhaps there is a special scholarship that only you are qualified to receive as a result of your circumstances that you view as a setback. Is there a frustrating element in your life that allows you to receive unique considerations and benefits? You may be familiar with the concept that people with blindness have other senses that are heightened. No, these people cannot see, but as a result of not being able to see, their hearing is more acute, they are incredibly tactile, and they are very perceptive.

When you find yourself feeling down about where life has placed you, take that list out and identify the advantage within that struggle. This will help to carry you a little further toward your end goal.

I would like to highlight a special person in my life that is working his inside track. Bobby Brown (my cousin), is the founder of Bobby Brown's Violence Prevention Initiatives. This is a non-profit organization that he established after he was shot and paralyzed in a drive-by shooting before his sophomore year in high school. He was not and is not involved in gang activity of any kind. He is a victim of senseless gun violence. Not only does his organization help to raise awareness of gun violence (celebrating over ten years of violence prevention outreach and service to the Twin Cities community), but he has also devoted his professional career as a psychotherapist to working with individuals and families. He is working to change the lives of people who could end up on either side of a gun if it were not for his efforts. His work is an example of leveraging a heartbreak and transforming its outcome into a positive impact. He is one of the reasons that I know I can make it. When his life changed forever, as a result of this tragic incident, he had a choice to make. He could have allowed this situation to paralyze his mind as well, but he didn't. I know first hand because I saw him in his hospital bed after the incident, maintaining light, as life as he once knew it was about to change forever. In the days following his discharge from the hospital, I watched him as he was in his bedroom unable to get up physically without assistance. While at times he was broken by despair, he still offered love to those around him. Weeks later I would see him every day at school learning; and while he was adjusting to his new life in a wheelchair, he was spreading hope to the entire student body through his smile, laugher, and inspiring message. Years later I would observe him at his basketball camp advocating for violence prevention. What a profound demonstration of tenacity his spirit has displayed! What a heroic human being he became that tragic day! While I am so clear the day-to-day struggle of living paralyzed is heartbreaking, I also know he chooses not to allow his physical state to dictate his future outcomes. You can take my body (temporarily), but you can't take my mind. He is married to one of the most beautiful women alive, and she has her head on straight as well. He is an inspiration, and his life shows that when life attempts to strip you of your ability to move forward, turn life on its head and push even harder and stronger by transforming your circumstances into opportunities!

FOUR
PACE YOURSELF

In track and field, there are different types of races. There are sprints, and there are long-distance runs. Having run track, I was taught that there are different approaches required when running each race based upon the type of race it is.

When you are leveraging who you are and where you want to go (staying in your lane) and exploiting your talents and abilities while doing so (working your inside track), you must pace yourself for the long run. Obviously, knowing the type of race you are in is how you determine which strategy to apply when running. In long-distance runs, the only way to get to the end is to pace yourself for the journey. The long-distance run is where we often find ourselves. While there are times in life when the paths we find ourselves on might lead us somewhere quickly, more often than not, anything worth having takes some time to achieve. Thus, you certainly can't afford to run a marathon at sprint speed. To get to life's finish line, which is always a long-distance run, you must pace yourself. That means that you are running with the understanding that you will not get to your goal quickly. As a result, you must conserve your energy where necessary in order to get all the way there.

In track and field, pacing yourself requires

two key strategies. The first strategy in pacing yourself is to breathe. Although your day-to-day engagement in life does not require thoughtful breathing, there are those times when the level of physical, mental, or emotional stress demands of you to take an intentional breath. Being intentional about that breath means you are not just focused on getting to your goal, but you are trying to get there in reasonable condition. If you are not cognizant about taking that breath you may forget to breathe at all. Forgetting to breathe does not necessarily mean you will stop breathing, but that is certainly possible. Forgetting to breathe undoubtedly means you will run your race far less effectively. The level of intention and strategy in breathing that is necessary in pacing yourself is comparable to women in labor. In order to get to the delivery of the baby, doctors and midwives recommend that you apply a breathing technique (thoughtfully breathing) throughout the labor so as to be able to manage the contractions and the duration of your labor. Let's face it, there are some things you can get away with not trying to breathe through, but there are some things that you just won't get through if you don't take that moment! If you do attempt to forego a breathing strategy, you will find yourself winded, exhausted, and defeated.

The second key strategy to pacing yourself is going the correct speed. In that long-distance run, trying to do it too quickly will get you nowhere fast. Then again, running too slowly will not allow you to build any momentum. There is an art to running a long-distance race. Monitoring your speed is about being honest about how much you have to work with (energy, strength, tenacity, and so on) and how far you have to go with what you have (exactly how long the race is). Money may be the simplest way to illustrate this point. Let's say you only have a hundred dollars to make it through the week. You may want to believe you can rush to spend without thinking things through, but you would be wise to consider the limitations that amount of money requires of you. So going the correct speed is integral to getting to the end. My point in all of this is for you to understand that pacing yourself may not seem as gratifying as getting there quickly. However, the way we are best able to sustain our victories is to have thoughtfully and purposefully walked out each step. If you are really trying to get there, then you have to be honest about the fact that there is only so much energy, money, time, and so on to go around, and as a result you should budget accordingly. Let's delve a little further into my husband's journey to extract the value in pacing yourself.

STORY | PACE YOURSELF MY DEAR

My husband's story continues with him going on to attend Georgetown University School of Medicine. He received a health professions scholarship from the United States Air Force to pay for medical school. He read and worked countless hours day in and day out. He often forsook the fun and fellowship that he may have wanted to engage in for the focus and consistency required to eventually graduate from medical school. Along with school, he would have to pass his USMLE (United States Medical Licensing Exam) Step 1 exam, which required him to demonstrate the depth of his medical knowledge. On his first attempt at the Step 1 exam, he did not pass. He did not pass his second attempt either. Why? Not pacing himself was ultimately his downfall. You see, on his first attempt, he would only be allowed six days to study for his exam (as a result of having to leave for a military obligation) while the rest of his classmates had three months of summer break to study. So while he gave it his best shot to be prepared on the exam date, he would not hit the mark. He failed by ten points. Prior to his second attempt, his academic advisor told him that as a result of failing his first attempt he would only have three weeks to study if he wanted to graduate with his current class. And while that was more study time than he had on his first attempt, both of his preparation periods combined did not equal the three-month time period for which most students have to prepare. Because he wanted to graduate with his class, he took the test anyway. Unfortunately, on the second attempt he failed by three points. While he was sure to get up and try again a third time, he was now more clear than ever that passing this test would require a significant amount of concentrated preparation and energy, so he decided to focus exclusively on studying for this exam. The only way he would be able to give it the time it deserved was to take the remainder of the semester off from medical school (which so happened to be the three-month period necessary to prepare). Finally having the appropriate time available to study, he eventually passed the exam. My husband went on to graduate from Georgetown University School of Medicine. When he walked across the stage, he was handed his Medical Doctorate, and he became Dr. D. Christopher Steele, or rather, D. Christopher

Steele, M.D.

Now, it can always be argued that someone else may have passed that test with less preparation time. However, it is far more effective when you are attempting to conquer something of great importance and significance that is integral to your goals, that you are clear on what gives you your best probability of finding success in that matter. We all know that haste makes waste; so while in theory you can accomplish many things hastily, you would be wise to pace yourself, which gives you the best odds of successful completion and of efficiently utilizing your resources.

The point behind all of this is to give yourself the extra juice you need to continue the journey, by more thoughtfully approaching the journey as a whole. It is taking those breaths and carefully monitoring your speed during the race that keeps you going and gets you to the end. Use this strategy where you believe it fits in your life. Here are some helpful ways that will allow you to pace yourself on your journey:

- *Budget your time and energy.* Yes, financial budgeting is important, but budgeting your time and energy is just as important. You owe it to yourself to be reasonable about how you allocate these most precious assets.

- *Do the things that help center you, bring you peace, and achieve a clearer headspace.* Go to church, a retreat, or a yoga class. Pray, meditate, and so on. A clear headspace is a must for a long journey.

- *Take special time for yourself to either do nothing or to do something that you love doing.* Treat yourself. Feed your spirit. This may be a spa day or a walk outside. Whatever you do, make it something that is extra special to you, and make it a regular part of your life. You won't make the distance if you don't give back to yourself.

- *Celebrate the little victories you get each day.* This allows you to not place so much focus on how far away you are from your goal; it allows you to place more emphasis on the glories that you will encounter before your end point.

- *Know that life sometimes happens much differently than anticipated.* This will assist you in coping with some of your unexpected life experiences because you have internalized that life often doesn't go as planned.

- *Don't try and chase everything at once.* In no way am I looking to discourage your aspiration toward multiple victories. Kudos to you! I am only suggesting you be mindful of the limitations you are working within, whatever they may be, so as to facilitate your successful arrival at all of your goals.

Pace yourself for the long run, my friend, because you may have a ways to go before you get there. However, the beauty of life is that sometimes life can surprise you, and just when you think you have to run another lap, you realize you finally made it.

FIVE
DON'T LOOK BACK

Have you ever tried to drive a car looking backward? (Aside from when you are intending to reverse.) Looking backward when driving in reverse is a phenomenal approach. However, if you are looking to go forward, I would suggest you keep your eyes on the road ahead. We have all had our share of experiences, setbacks, disappointments, or even victories in our past; and while it is always useful to use each of these to set the stage for the future, it is also important to keep your sights set forward on the goal.

In track and in life, looking back only slows you down. It makes you more inclined to enter someone else's lane or change your pace because of the speed you see someone else going. Looking back can leave you paralyzed by yesterday's victories that make you feel like today's failure. Looking back can leave you stagnant as you are so focused on a past mistake that you don't see the opportunities for growth and success ahead of you. Looking back can have you all tripped up and not utilizing the energy you need to move forward most effectively. Let's use celebrity culture as an example. There are many examples you may be able to recall about those who had a bright and shining moment at one point in their careers. I am talking the kind of moment that is difficult to top, given its magnitude and significance. It is often said to be a once-in-a-lifetime kind of moment; and while this level of success may be achieved again, it might not be. You may be able to think of an instance or two of a celebrity who seems to be chasing that moment from the past, and as a result doesn't get much further. While chasing anything may seem like forward movement, directing the chase forward is the only way to advance. Looking back while trying to go forward is not much different than going backward.

Another way we may find ourselves looking back is related to our toughest moments. Now, allow me to clarify that I think it is important to use your experiences to propel you forward in life, but placing the wrong level of emphasis on a past hurt, bad experience, and so on can be debilitating to your future. There are examples all over the place of people who just can't seem to get past the heartache to move forward into the future. For example, people who found love and lost it and have been unable to get into a new relationship over a significant period of time. Every person who comes into their life as an opportunity for a new relationship is only a reminder of the love they lost. Let me be clear, I have had my share of experiences that have left me paralyzed and focused on the past, but I, too, have to accept how that only slows me down. Life can be heartbreaking. Life is not always nice to you. However, you owe it to yourself to focus your attention on the opportunities ahead and get to your end goal.

I would like to share a story with you of a young man who has a lot of reasons to want to look back, but he has advanced in life as a result of his looking forward.

STORY | THE YOUNG MAN WITH ONLY ONE EYE TO LOOK BACK

I once knew a young boy with the courage of a champion. Why do I say the courage of a champion? Let me explain. On April 5, 1984, a beautiful, vibrant little boy was born. He was born to two lovely parents. This was their second child. Somewhere around the first year of this child's life the mother began to notice her son was running into walls. She discerned that something was wrong. She often raised this issue with his doctor and medical staff at the clinic, but she was told her son's behaviors were typical of his development stage, and he would outgrow them. One day the mother was more certain than ever that something was wrong with her son. As she looked him in the eyes, she was able to see straight through his right eye. She was obviously alarmed, and very quickly everything changed. This baby's retina had detached itself from the eye, and he was diagnosed with retinoblastoma (cancer of the eye) at fifteen months old. This was a terribly heartbreaking experience for the parents. Can you even imagine? The doctors informed the parents that it would be necessary to remove the baby's right eye in order to get rid of the cancer. In spite of the parents' prayers for this to not be the outcome, it was. Not only that, but the doctors also recommended chemotherapy to help prevent the cancer from returning. The baby went on to have eye removal surgery, and the doctors inserted a port in his chest that would facilitate chemotherapy if the parents agreed to it. The parents and their pastor prayed and came to the collective decision to not go through with the chemotherapy. The mother asked the doctors if the chemotherapy would ensure the cancer would not return, but the doctors could not make that claim. So this baby would endure a surgery that included the removal of the port (which left a scar that remains on his chest to this day). Every three months, for the next seven years, this child would endure spinal taps, CT scans, and bone marrow biopsies. The parents and I had to manage the heartbreak of watching him scream in the hospital bed while he was being rolled off to the operating room for these procedures. This champion is my brother, and he is undoubtedly a survivor. Let's pause for a moment and acknowledge the heartbreak, challenge, and courage on the part of my parents who lived courageously through their child having such an experience.

My brother grew up to be a man who did not face cancer again, but he faced a series of other challenges. Some of the challenges he faced would come as a result of living life with one eye. As my brother and I were growing up, I watched him endure the trauma associated with having one eye. He was teased, called names, and ridiculed for an attribute he had no control over. He was constantly reminded of the limitations having one eye granted him. From his attempts to pass his driver's license exam (which required a vision test where you are instructed to cover each eye and read the letters revealed), to simply sitting next to someone he is unable to see without turning his head (if they happened to be on his right side). He would have to live his day-to-day life in a survival mode that few could ever begin to understand. You can just about imagine the courage it takes for him not to look back on the experience of losing an eye and allow it to dictate what he will and won't go after. Do you think he let having only one eye stop him? Of course not! He ran track and field and placed eighth in the nation in the Junior Olympics. He received all-conference honors in football in high school, was awarded an athletic scholarship to the University of North Dakota, played arena football professionally, and was scouted and offered tryouts by NFL teams. On April 5, 2010 (his birthday) he worked out for the Carolina Panthers. He considered this experience to be a divine gift. Ultimately, he did not receive an offer to play for this team, but this workout, having taken place on the anniversary of his birth, satisfied his NFL dream and gave him the solace he desired to move on to other dreams and pursuits outside of being a professional athlete. Recently his undergraduate alma mater acknowledged him as fourth all-time in sacks for the university. You would imagine if he looked back (if he considered for a moment that he only had one eye) he would have never gotten out there to play sports in the first place. He is currently a student at the University of North Dakota Law School and Business School, as he was accepted into their Juris Doctorate and Master of Business Administration program. He has established notoriety through music, athleticism, and through his entrepreneurial spirit. He is continuing to race toward new dreams even today. Not looking back on the experience of having lost an eye, but looking forward with his sights set on the possibilities of the future. I couldn't be prouder of my brother's strength and determination, which led him to be the exceptional human being he is today.

The moral of the story is, don't look back. Looking back won't get you much further. Looking back will only reveal you may be moving in reverse. Looking back will leave you frustrated with today because you are assessing it in reference to yesterday. Although all of us experience tragedies and triumphs that are great, they don't make us exempt from the impact of focusing our attention behind us when we are trying to move ahead. You have got to move forward with a clear focus on the road ahead, taking the lessons learned from your past experiences, but proceeding forward with a clarity and intention that is only possible when you don't look back.

SIX
FINISH STRONG

Finishing strong is probably the concept that is easiest to explain and hardest to execute. Finishing strong may not always be the obvious approach to the runner in the race. When you have been in a long run, and you have likely lost most of the energy and fervor you may have had at the beginning, sometimes finishing any way you can is all you care about. And by the way, I totally get that. Finishing the race is a feat unto itself, and it deserves some glory. My thought, however, is that when you already know the gold medal is not up ahead (because you may not be advancing as quickly), you must engage in your own personal race toward what you feel you are still able to achieve as a result of finishing. For example, maybe you were unable to graduate with your fellow classmates, but graduating is still of importance to you. For you it is not important to place your focus on when you finish, but that you do! Not only that, but also recognizing that you are not the one ahead; how do you handle such an experience? Do you think everything you did was in vain? Did you become bitter? The race is only a waste if you can't finish it with grace. You can always feel good about your having run in the race as long as you finish strong. Finishing strong is about giving the end everything you've got. This means that giving it your all is not contingent upon you knowing the outcome will be favorable. You give it all you've got simply because you are in the race.

Let me explain this another way. In track and field there are two applicable concepts: the sprint finish and the photo finish. The sprint finish is about a sudden increase in intensity toward the end of the race. This is where you have to dig deep by pulling up all of the energy you have left to kick things into high gear. The photo finish is referring to the camera at the finish line that captures how you come through that line. This is how it is best determined who actually won and who didn't. I was always taught to lean into the finish line for the photo finish. This means that while from one angle it may look as if your competitor won, the photo finish may reveal a different result. Now let's think for a moment about life's proverbial photo finish. You are being watched by others who admire you, by God (depending on your beliefs), by haters, and by others. How do you want to be captured going through the finish line? As one who is pouting because everything didn't work out as you had anticipated, or as one who is inspiring others to finish with grace even if you don't get to win the race? Finishing strong is when you gather up every ounce of anything you have left to make it through the finish line and still maintain your character, your brilliance, and your light. Finishing strong is about showing that you can look beyond the obvious win and see the true victory of completing the feat. Finishing strong is all about your willpower, determination, and ferocity. It is mirrored in the example of Martin Luther King Jr.'s life, which he ended still maintaining the virtues of fighting for freedom without violence, even though his eyes were not able to see his dream realized as he crossed the finish line. Finishing strong is about the courage, strength, and wisdom that keeps you striding into the finish line as if you had a shot at winning the gold, even when you know you don't. After all, what was the whole point of the race if you don't follow it through to the very end with the same willpower it took to start the race? So I admonish you, my friend, finish strong. You may have to locate your victory in life's unexpected places. Sometimes that is the only motivation you will have to finish at all. All of this will allow you to run through that finish line with a grace and light that indicates you were the true winner anyway. I will continue with my husband's story, which is a beautiful illustration of finishing strong.

STORY | DR. STEELE'S STRONG RESIDENCY FINISH

Dr. Steele was accepted into an exceptional residency program for pediatrics at what was once called the National Naval Medical Center. It seemed that Dr. Steele's strides had finally paid off for him, in that he was now about to focus on his area of specialization in medicine. He was the first black male to be granted entry into the residency program in over ten years. Dr. Steele focused and worked hard, day in and day out. However, he ran into a few major roadblocks on his path. He was doing well in his outpatient rotations (a month of practicum work and hands-on training in a specific area of focus in a clinic setting). However, when he would finish an ICU (Intensive Care Unit) rotation having received positive verbal feedback from the attending (senior medical doctor in charge), he would later learn that he didn't pass the rotation and would have to repeat it. This occurred regularly. In spite of him consistently being given glowing reviews in person, he would later learn he didn't get a positive written review. There was, however, one very consistent statement made regarding Dr. Steele in his written reviews. It was that he always had a great attitude. The attendings would often remark that he had the most incredible spirit and energy. This was something he brought to the experience beyond the other performance markers. It didn't matter how many times they sent him back to repeat a rotation, he maintained a gracious spirit. At this point, challenge and adversity were nothing new to Dr. Steele. Every rotation they required him to repeat, he did it with a level of class. On top of that, Dr. Steele would have to pass his Step 3 exam (demonstrating his depth in medical knowledge) during his time in the program. He took his Step 3 exam on two occasions, passing the exam on the second time. However, all of the delays his past rotation outcomes created and the initial unsuccessful test outcome eventually led Dr. Steele to a probation status in the residency program, which eventually led to his being terminated from the program after completing two and a half years of a three-year residency. Now that hurts!

But my point isn't that he was unable to complete the program; my point is how he finished. I personally sat with him through the probation hearings that included a room full of fifteen to twenty high-ranking military medical officers speaking of my husband as if he were incompetent and mentally handicapped (I am not saying that to be dramatic –

this really happened). I am so serious. We had these hearings to attend that led up to his termination from the program, and they spoke of him as if he wasn't sitting right in the room. I must say, it took everything in me not to have an outburst. What I was most struck by was how he handled it. And it wasn't an act, because I went home with him. He would sit through those hearings as they drug his name through the mud, and he would literally smile and respond with virtue and grace. It takes a mighty BIG man to sit through people treating him as if he is so small. How did he finish strong? Well, he ended his experience in that program with a level of grace up until the very last moment, and I am so grateful to have witnessed it firsthand. He is an amazing human being. And guess what else? He earned his due. As a result of working as a flight surgeon in the United States Air Force (the work he did after his strong finish in the residency program), he now has the option to become board certified in occupational medicine and/or aerospace medicine if he so chooses. He served as Interim Chief of Aerospace Medicine and will soon obtain the official position as Chief of Aerospace Medicine. When one door closed, life offered him a window that he climbed right through and kept moving forward. No, he didn't get to complete his residency. However, he did everything in his power up until the bitter end to finish strong, and in doing so, he completed it with class!

My people, I encourage you to finish strong. Whatever you may be pursuing. This finishing-strong notion is about maintaining your grace under fire. It is about being a good sport. It is about demonstrating that you don't have to be the person to get the gold to be the person with the good attitude. I always love it when they end the various games in sports by having the teams shake hands. One of those teams is on the losing side. And although the winning team deserves its moment and gets one, that losing team shines bright by having such grace under a less than desirable outcome. It is also important to state that finishing strong is not just about maintaining grace when you lose; it is also about maintaining grace when you win. The grace is who you are; the outcome is simply the outcome.

I admonish you, my people, let's all finish strong. Let's be the type of people who shine our light in spite of the outcome. You will have some false starts, but remember, you have to get back out there in the race! You might find yourself distracted, but you have got to stay in your lane! You have got to

work your inside track to bring you close to your goal!
You have to remember to pace yourself, as life is
always a long-distance run! Don't you dare look back!
Keep your eyes on the road ahead! Run your race like
no one else can! So whatever the case may be,
wherever life may lead you, when you are
approaching that finish line, go ahead and do your
thing—finish strong!

CONCLUSION
PASS THE BATON

Remembering to pass the baton is one of the most important aspects of running your race. While you personally will benefit from the races you run in life, there are some races that will also benefit those who are following in your footsteps. Passing the baton is about remembering that there are those who will come after you who may get to behold the glory of the victories your eyes may never see. Passing the baton is about understanding that you are running for you *and* for your people. Who are your people? Your people may be your children or grandchildren. Your people may be your relatives or friends. Your people may be your co-workers or employees. Your people may even be the next generation. Whatever the case may be, you must run the race not only with your own victories in mind, but run your race knowing that your victories today may lead to tomorrow's victories for another. Passing the baton is about being intentional in your efforts and decisions because you have the future in mind. Passing the baton is about understanding you may not be the one to get the gold medal, but you are currently touching the baton that will lead your people to victory.

I am reminded of many of the examples in history and in my life of the people who used their journeys to fight for the victories of not just themselves, but for others. I would like to honor my father and mother for passing the baton to me and helping to teach me the importance of paying it forward:

- *Alfred Babington-Johnson*, M.Div., President and CEO of the Stairstep Initiative Companies. His foundation, Stairstep Foundation, is a community-building organization that focuses on reaching back in order to bring others forward. "Stairstep was formed in 1992 as a God-inspired response to a set of awesome challenges that confronted society at large and African-Americans, in particular" (stairstep.org). I believe in contributing to my community and to others as a result of my father's example and work. I am an entrepreneur and will continue to find new successes in business because of my father's entrepreneurial example; he has received national accolades in business. Ironically, one of his companies was mentioned in a textbook I was required to read in one of my business classes at Howard University. I attended Howard University as a result of my father's contagious excitement for his alma mater that rubbed off on me. I am committed to helping others go further as a result of his commitment to advancing the lives of others. This book would not exist were it not for his ability to extract the *"RUN YOUR RACE!"* story from my life and highlight it for me throughout my journey when I needed it most.

- *Denise L. Smith*, Educator (Master of

Curriculum and Instruction & Master of Administration and Supervision). For over two decades she has worked in education with a strong commitment to bringing out excellence in her students. She has worked not only as an educator, but also as an administrator. She uses affirmations, poetry, and songs to inspire her students to not only get book smart, but to get heart smart as well. Throughout my life, my mother raised me to be strong and to believe in myself. I wouldn't have written this book without her speaking it into my life prior to its inception. She is my strength, and she is my model of how to overcome any obstacle and rise like a phoenix from the ashes. She has dealt with hardships unimaginable throughout her life and has not allowed them to deter her. She is my example of strength, courage, and undeniable beauty (inside and out).

Now allow me to pass the baton to you by sharing with you the things I use to help me keep going through my toughest times.

Resources and strategies I use to keep me going:

- The live broadcast of The Potter's House worship service or *The Potter's Touch* broadcast (tdjakes.org).

- *Super Soul Sunday* (the OWN Network).

- Poems: "Mother to Son" and "Dreams" by Langston Hughes (I have these poems committed to memory).

- Songs: "The Climb" by Miley Cyrus; "Hello" by T.I. feat. Cee Lo Green; "Survive" by Mary Mary; "Diamond" by Rihanna; "Can't Tell Me Nothing" by Kanye West; "Superpower" by Beyoncé; "I Made It" by Jay Z; "It Will All Be Worth It" by Mary Mary; "Happy" by Pharrell Williams (one of my husband's favorites); "Flawless" by Beyoncé; "Sweeter Tomorrow" by Germane Champagne feat. Margeaux, and tons of other music from a variety of genres that inspire me, keep me going, get me hyped, or help me focus.

- Bible: Philippians 4:13, 2 Corinthians 4:8–

10, Psalm 91, Romans 8 (highlighting verses 18, 31–39), Psalm 27, Galatians 6:9, and other scriptures about faith, hope, and courage in the face of adversity.

- Read a stimulating book by an author such as Malcolm Gladwell, Seth Godin, or myself (wink).

- Watch a cerebral documentary such as *Bloomberg Game Changers*, *Happy*, et cetera.

- Go for a good bike ride! I ride in defiance of the weather conditions—that makes it all the more liberating for me. Be wise though. If the meteorologist is warning you to stay inside, please do so until the weather clears up!

- Do whatever I (you) feel like doing (within reason)!

So when life wears you down, as it has a way of doing, apply the strategies in this book and RUN YOUR RACE!

ACKNOWLEDGEMENTS

Thanks be to God, without whom I could do nothing. There is no possible way I would have made it this far without You! Thank You for transforming my life through the very thing that was intended to take me out—You intended it for good. Special thanks to: Dwayne (my rock), you really are the wind beneath my wings! Mom (my strength), you are love and beauty personified! Dad (my hero), you are the most humble, generous, caring, and wise spirit I know! Z (my heart), you are such a bright and shiny spirit—a star! Bobby, you are a warrior! Thank you all for generously allowing me to share aspects of your lives to paint this beautiful picture, my first book! Thank you, Jill Amack and Menia Buckner (Aunt Menia) for providing your incredible editing services!

Thanks to Big E (your royal highness), Poppa Steele, Grandma Neblett, Grandma Nina and Uncle Sonny, Momma Anna, TaMica' (Christina, Christopher, Savannah, Flora and Calvin), Deon, Danielle and Romain, Dave and family, Tifphanie, Raichel, the Brown family, the Crosbys (Meredith, Brian, and Noah), Aunt Della, Aunt Fay, Dr. Battle, all of my Grace Temple Deliverance Center family, First Assembly of God Church in Alexandria, to my girls (Stephanie, Kristian, Adrienne, and Lindsey), the Funbunch, Paul Hatch, Paul Wharton (I will love you forever!), Derrick Holmes, Parisa, Tara, the Richardsons, the Brathwaites and to the many others (aunts, uncles, cousins, friends, loved ones, et cetera) I am unable to name. I wouldn't have made it this far without you all. You are oh, so dear to my heart!

Thank you Altru Grand Forks medical staff for

all that you have done on our family's behalf. Special thanks to Dr. Wildey and Erin Wevers, R.N.—you are amazing! Thank you Rebekah Knapp for your midwifery care and for your commitment to my natural birth experience. Thank you Altru Foundation for the beautiful work you do to honor families in bereavement. Thank you Dahl Funeral Home staff. Thank you 319th Medical Group for all of your support towards my husband and me. Thank you Peggy Littlefield for the childcare education you provided me during my pregnancy.

Thank you Dakota Sky for giving me the strength to be transparent and for being the reason I know I am a force to be reckoned with! I adore you! Dominic, I can't wait for you to arrive—Dakota's beautiful spirit will continue through you.

www.ingramcontent.com/pod-product-compliance
Lightning Source LLC
LaVergne TN
LVHW021359080426
835508LV00020B/2350